Independence
Day

by Natalie Goldstein

PEARSON

Scott
Foresman

Editorial Offices: Glenview, Illinois • Parsippany, New Jersey • New York, New York
Sales Offices: Needham, Massachusetts • Duluth, Georgia • Glenview, Illinois
Coppell, Texas • Ontario, California • Mesa, Arizona

The Colonies Want to Be Free

In 1776 every American lived in one of thirteen colonies. The colonies were ruled by England. Americans, however, wanted the **freedom** to rule their own country.

Men from each **colony** went to a meeting. Five of those men wrote the Declaration of Independence. This paper said the country was free. On July 4, the men at this meeting accepted this paper.

The Declaration of Independence

Most of the Delcaration of Independence was written by Thomas Jefferson. Americans liked his ideas about freedom so much that July 4 has become a big **holiday**.

Thomas Jefferson

The signing of the Declaration of Independence

Fighting for Freedom

The colonists had an army to fight the English for their freedom. George Washington was the general who led the army. After years of fighting, the colonists won. America was free!

After the war Washington became the first **President** of the United States.

George Washington

The First Independence Day

The Fourth of July was first celebrated in 1777 in Philadelphia. This celebration had a parade, music, the firing of a cannon, and fireworks.

Cannons and fireworks were fired on July 4, 1777.

Fireworks on the Fourth

Americans from all over liked fireworks. In 1800 **citizens** of New York City celebrated Independence Day with fireworks. Fireworks exploded in different colors. They went high into the sky and burst into beautiful lights.

Americans loved the fireworks. In 1805 Boston also celebrated Independence Day with fireworks. Soon other places also celebrated the day with fireworks.

Americans celebrate the Fourth of July with fireworks.

Celebrating Today

Today, Americans celebrate the Fourth of July with parades. Many parades have bands that play music. Some people dress up in fancy costumes or dance and carry banners. Other people cheer and wave flags.

At night people go to see fireworks. Americans have fun celebrating the Fourth of July.

People celebrate the Fourth of July with parades.

Glossary

citizen a member of a state and country

colony a place that is ruled by a country that is far away

freedom a person's right to make choices

holiday a special day

President our country's leader